ISBN 978-0-483-68157-6
PIBN 10435797

A Lovers' Knot

An Opera in One Act

The Book by
Cora Bennett-Stephenson

The Music by
Simon Buchhalter

Vocal Score
Price, $2.50 net

G. Schirmer

London · New York · Boston

FIRST PERFORMANCE

AT THE

AUDITORIUM THEATER, CHICAGO

January 15, 1916

CAST OF CHARACTERS

Sylvia	Myrna Sharlow
Beatrice	Augusta Lenska
Walter	George Hamlin
Edward	Graham Marr

Conductor_____Marcel Charlier

Staged by Désiré Defrère

Scene: A Garden in front of Edward's house, Norfolk, Virginia.

Time: About 1870.

Story of the Opera

Walter, a young Virginia gentleman, has traveled for a long time, vainly attempting to forget his love for Beatrice. He does not believe she loves him, but fears she would consent to marry him because his father, during the Civil War, rescued her father from the battle-field at the cost of his own life. At the time Walter returns from his travels, Beatrice is entertaining a Northern friend, Sylvia, who loves and is loved by Edward, Beatrice's brother and bosom friend of Walter. At the first meeting between Walter and Sylvia, both Beatrice and her brother mistake Walter's natural courtesy toward Sylvia for love, and whereas Edward decides to give Sylvia up to Walter, Beatrice cannot decide to give Walter up to Sylvia. Sylvia, suspecting what is wrong with Beatrice, confesses her love for Edward, whereupon Beatrice tells of her love for Walter.

Sylvia then disguises herself as a man and makes violent love to Beatrice, who is cleverly dressed so as to pass for either Sylvia or herself. This scene is enacted in sight of both Edward and Walter, each of whom believes the object of his affections duped by a vile adventurer; they interrupt the love-making, and thus discover the ruse, which ends as the plotters intended it should, Walter proposing to Beatrice and Edward claiming the object of his affection, Sylvia.

To Mr. Charles G. Dawes

A Lovers' Knot

Opera in One Act

Scene I

The Book by
Cora Bennett-Stephenson

The Music by
Simon Buchhalter

26778

attacca subito

Allegro vivace

8

Curtain II Curtain goes up quickly

12

The scene is a beautiful informal flower-garden with two trees. Under the tree at left centre there are wicker chairs and a table, on which has been placed a shallow basket filled with spools of gay colored silk thread. There stands beside the table an embroidery frame over which is stretched a rose-colored web with a design of gold thread in lovers' knots, none of them completed. The other tree is at right up-stage. Around its first, low fork is built a crow's-nest with steps, rail and a seat of rustic woodwork. This crow's-nest gives prospect down an avenue apparently leading from the garden.

Beatrice is discovered working at the embroidery.

Moderato

(impatiently)

(Beatrice fastens the needle in the cloth and

I'll sew no   more!

herself affectionately on the arm of Beatrice's chair and leaning over to examine the embroidery)

Moderato

f

mf espressivo

begins tying threads on the underside)

marcato

Horn

Allegro moderato

The needle cuts the thread.

Sylvia (playfully)

The lambrequin's un-finish'd —   I-dle girl!

Allegro moderato

I'll

p   *mf*

cantabile

Why should my hands be cold, my fore-head warm? Why should I

sleep a-way the beau - - teous night?

Allegro moderato

Allegro moderato
con passione

(boldly)

Pray tell me

Agitato

(pretending scorn) *mf*

In love! You fool-ish girl! In love! You have lost your

love!

Agitato

Andante

wits!

(with feeling)

On-ly my heart, my Be - a - trice! My wits I

Andante

espressivo

(Beatrice drops her mask, obviously interested)

Your heart?

do re-tain. I've on - ly ___ lost my heart!

Are you in love?_____ (Sylvia nods her head

Allegro agitato

affirmatively. She suddenly paces up and down restlessly, and stops)

Allegro agitato

ppp subito

Allegro agitato

(with agitation) *mf*

My fore-head burns like yours, my

Allegro agitato

cresc. *ff* *p*

hands are cold as ice! You are so deep in love,

Moderato

you do not see I nei-ther sleep nor eat, I dream the

Allegro

live-long day.

Arioso

"There lived near us a neighbor's son"

(brightly) *mf*

A wo-man grown ___ I craved his love, His strength made sweet with ten-der-ness.

(forlornly) *p*

A-las! A-las!

(more and more agitated) *mf*

There came a day,

that dear, last day, As was his wont to vis-it me! The

(with ecstasy and pointing towards the blooming flowers)

gar - den breathed a spell; 'twas Spring,— like

this! The birds all sang of

love, so full of bliss.

The flow'rs their per-fume shed for in-cense rare. He took my hand! I felt his love thrill through me, Then the rash-est, fond-est words e'er said but trem-bled on his lips.

(as if lost in memory) rit. Tempo Iº (rousing herself)

Per - haps e - ven now thy lov - er turns_ towards

(Beatrice is seized with a rapture of sudden hope)

rit. Presto

towards home and me,_____ towards home and me!

home!_____

(With enthusiasm Sylvia catches Beatrice by the hand, and they sing in a spirited manner)

Duet

"Love laughs at Fate's grim barriers"

Presto

king,   for   Love   is   king!

king,   for   Love   is   king!

For   Love   is

king!

For Love is king!

Love to the world his chal-lenge throws,

Love to the

Love to the world his chal-lenge throws,

world his chal-lenge throws, his ban

his ban - - - ner flings, his

38

For Love is king!

For Love is king!

Moderato

Love   reigns in gra - cious   ma - jes-

Love   reigns in gra - cious   ma - jes-

ty till Death doth part; Love

ty till Death doth part; Love

from the hurt of Ty - rant Time

from the hurt of Ty - rant Time

shall keep the heart.

shall keep the heart.

accel. poco a poco

(They rouse themselves, and with a lively dance - - - - - -

accel. poco a poco

accel. poco a poco

- - - they stop at centre of stage and sing)

f tr (ad lib.)

Ah! _____ for

f tr (ad lib.)

Ah! _____ for

Allegro moderato

Love yields to love, if love____ be__ love,____ and my

Love yields to love, if love____ be__ love,____ and my

Allegro moderato

Edward (enters, flourishing a letter)

I bring good news!

We shortly en-ter-

tain___ a welcome guest!

(emotionally)

A guest? Speak! Who?

Our Wal - ter!

Moderato

(Thrusts letter into Beatrice's hands; she eagerly seizes it; but does not read it; she seems

Read!

overcome with conflicting emotions)

44

Beatrice (aside, with feeling)

Are my___ un - rest, my quick - ened___ need,___

are my___ un - rest, my quick - ened need, true pro - - phe -

cies?

(Goes slowly off stage, holding letter to her heart. During this time Edward and Sylvia exchange

26778

greetings and whisper while watching Beatrice leave the stage)

dim.

p

dim. e rit.

pp

attacca subito

Scene: Sylvia and Edward

Sylvia seats herself before the embroidery frame with a coquettish glance at Edward, which he takes as per-
mission to seat himself on the grass beside her. After waiting a little time he takes the end of her sash to
fondle it. During all this time Sylvia stitches daintily.

Presto

p accel.

Moderato

Sylvia (with decision)

Who   is Wal-ter,   pray?

(Edward kisses the end of Sylvia's sash)

Moderato

fp

(Sylvia shrugs her shoulders and signifies by facial

Edward (buoyantly)

Wal-ter is wa-ter that quench-es thirst,

mf

expression that she accepts his
mood and the charming evasion)

Wal - ter is bread in the land of Fam - ine!

(Stimulated by a look of encouragement, Edward assumes a gay, enigmatical air)

Of all my_ friends he shall al - ways be first, of

all   my   friends   he

Allegro vivace   (Sylvia resumes sewing)   **Moderato**

And   what   is   my   rank,

shall al-ways be   first!

Sir?   And what my de - gree,   in the most   no - ble peerage of friend -

(Sylvia, after a flash

friend-ship is sil - ver; you— you are gold-en!

of a happy smile, appears to be intent on her
sewing to the exclusion of everything else)

Allegro vivace

Allegro vivace

accel.

(Takes great pains with her stitches and draws back from her work
with head poised sidewise to observe effect of her embroidery)

And now—

Moderato

S. Will you tell me, what this Wal - ter is like?

I__ am cu - rious.

Allegro

(Sylvia, with a sidelong,

(The expression of Edward's face turns from

You, curious?

coquettish glance, nods affirmation)

incredulity to disatisfaction and then to a look of mischief)

Then lis - ten!

Buffo Song
"I swear 'tis true"

(He ponders a moment, and then indicates by gesture that he will play a trick on Sylvia to punish her for her curiosity concerning a stranger.)

Allegro giocoso

ear!......

I swear 'tis true!......

I swear 'tis...... true! I swear 'tis

true! I swear 'tis true! I swear 'tis

true!

He o - gles la-dies fair, But he's too shy to woo them! He's writ a book of po - ems, But no one can con-strue them! He dreads a mouse, fears

eve-ning dew,   Be - lieves in_ dreams:_____

I swear 'tis   true!_____   I swear 'tis_   true!   I

swear 'tis_   true!   I swear 'tis   true!   I swear 'tis

true!   He

will not wear a sword, He swoons if he but see one; He rides a

don-key small! He's not con-tent to

be one! And yet— I think he will in-te-rest

you In spite of this:

R. I swear 'tis true! ____ I swear 'tis ___ true! I

R. swear 'tis ___ true! I swear 'tis true! I

R. swear 'tis true! ____ (Sylvia is astounded, but before she can

say anything Beatrice runs in)

Allegro vivace

Mesto

Wal-ter's brave sire, at call for re-treat,

Bear - ing— Fa - ther to safe - ty, fell

dead at his feet!

(vigorously)

Ed-ward and I have sworn e-ter-nal grat-i-tude,

(Sylvia is beset with conflicting emotions: a desire to respect the man Beatrice loves and a dislike of the picture drawn by Edward)

e - ter-nal grat - i - tude!

Edward (out of sight)

Here he is! It_ is real-ly

Allegro giocoso

Wal - ter!

(Enter Edward with Walter, who is in every respect the opposite of the picture drawn by Edward. Edward, after a roguish look toward Sylvia, assists Walter in laying aside traveling cloak. Sylvia, after a first gasp of surprise, recognizes that a joke has been played on her, and signifies that she will have speedy revenge. Walter kisses Beatrice's hand with grave tenderness)

Pompously

Moderato

Edward
(to Beatrice, rather gloomily)

(Spoken) Still so mys-te-rious?

He

does not men-tion why he went a - way.

Beatrice

Agitato

Edward (stricken with violent jealousy)

Beatrice (astounded at the suggestion)

(Walter and Sylvia attempt to seize the same spool but accidentally their hands are clasped for a single moment [at x])

See, when he smiles at her, Is he not a-dor-a-ble? Ah! love! — — —

He does not hear, he sees but her, He is in love — in love with Syl-vi-a!

He's known her but a

Walter (rousing himself with effort)

mf slower

I am trav-el-worn, and dust-y.

Beatrice (coming forward hospitably and pushing past Edward, who does not recover his composure so readily)

I hope you'll comfort find.

Edward (feigning composure)

Passionato con moto

Yes, come with me!

(Walter bows to Sylvia with a half-smile: gravely to Beatrice; Edward goes into the house, Walter lags behind while Sylvia and Beatrice go into garden out of sight)

Romanza

"To wander far away is vain"

78

26778

Ed - ward does not speak, I half sus - pect:

Allegro appassionato

I tease, e - vade:

In turn he doubts, and

hopes, But ends by keep - ing still!

Allegro moderato

But Walter's

S. still a mys-ter - y. There's something on his

mind! Could we but

find,_____ could we but find_____

what scru - ple says_____

Sylvia's Scheme

Tempo di Valse

(Sylvia looks in all directions to make sure she is not overheard)

you   the la - dy_ fair!   You_ will wear my

sky - blue_____ cloak   A - top_ your

gray print gown.   My feather - fan will

serve_ to mask_ your face   and nut - brown hair!

So will____ each youth sur - mise, His sweet - heart is an- oth - - ers! And thus per - haps he will feel the sor-row-joy of lov - - ers.

(Sylvia shakes off her gloom and Beatrice appears interested)

faith - ful heart it breaks!

*A

I will mouth the pledg - es sweet That

Ed - ward owes to me!

* For purposes of abbreviation the part A to B may be omitted.

24778

All is fair in love and war, and

this is lov — ing war!

(Beatrice smiles in sympathy)

* For purposes of abbreviation the part C to D may be omitted.

And— you must— be en - tranced as— I would

sure - ly be, If at my feet my dear

one, my dear one—— had laid his heart! And you will acqui - esce!

Ah!—— then I'll show you how I dream! I hope! I

Ah!____ for

(Beatrice catches the enthusiasm of Sylvia.)

Ah!____ for

Love yields to love, if love____ be____

Love yields to love, if love____ be____

26778

love, ___ and my love ___ is love! For love yields to

love, ___ and my love ___ is love! For love yields to

love if love be ___ love, ___ love ___

love if love be ___ love, ___ love ___

___ be love!

___ be love!

Curtain falls rapidly

Presto

Scene II

Prelude: "Love"

Allegro moderato

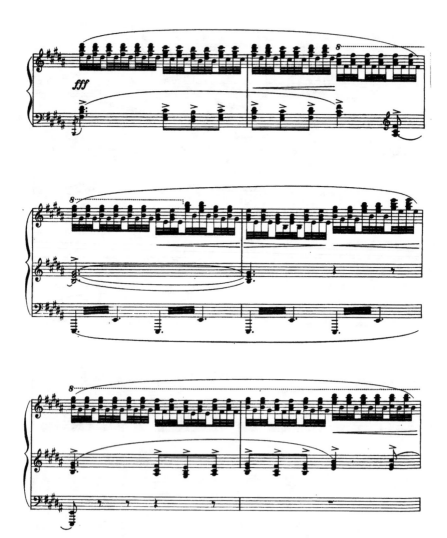

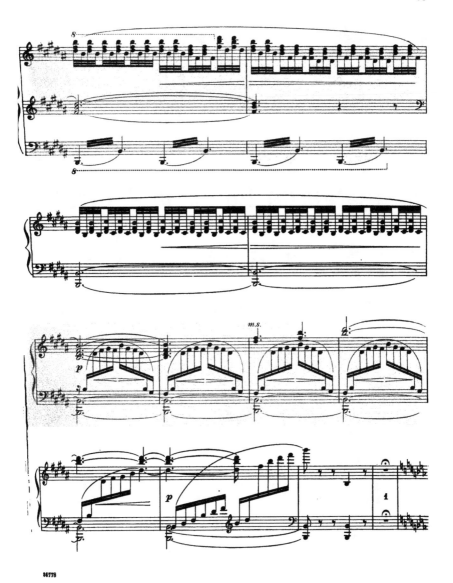

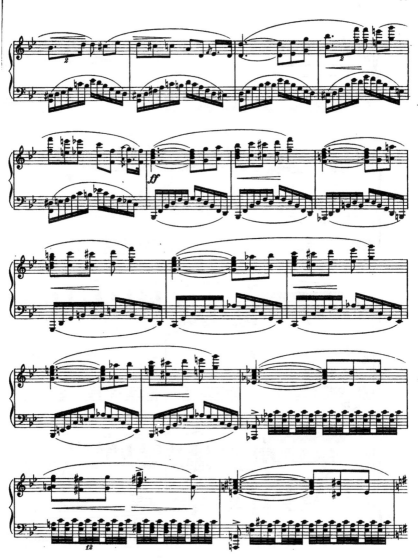

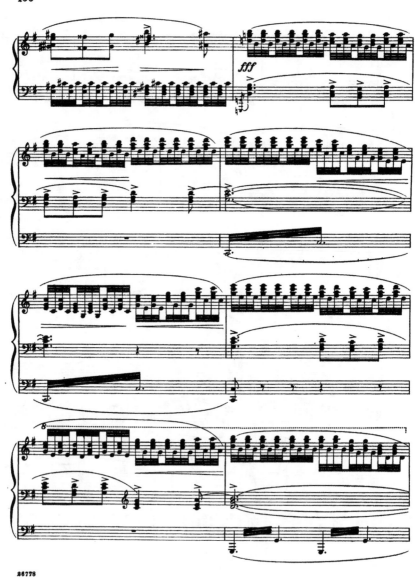

Allegro

(Curtain rises; Stage set as in Scene I)

(Enter Edward and Walter walking arm in arm. Walter has changed his traveling costume for a suit, cut according to the mode as given in Edward's costume; but the trousers and vest are white and the coat is plum-colored.

Moderato   **Allegro**   **Moderato**

Neither Walter nor Edward wears a hat.)

Edward

mf

If in our South-land lives the maid that won your heart's de - vo-tion,

(Walter's interruption is sudden and passionate, in sharp contrast to his previous restraint and gentle manner)

Allegro

Walter *f*

W.

mf

E.

Why did you wan-der far and long?

Allegro

(Sylvia, dressed as a charming youth and disguised by a blond wig, enters stealthily at rear. She is drawing along by the hand Beatrice, who wears the blue mantle belonging to Sylvia and who carries before her face, completely covering it, a large fan of black ostrich-feathers.)

(They slip up the step of the crow's-nest and take seats on the bench. After a few preliminary caresses, Sylvia drops on her knees and in pantomime plays the lover. All this time they are not observed by the two men. Walter meantime is carried back to the days of his happy dream with Beatrice. He grows tender and reminiscent.)

Aria
"To take again the little hand in mine"

No thought of du-ty then! She gave her child's pure heart

as free As per - fume, as per-fume breathes from out the rose, as

per - fume breathes from out the rose.

Tempo Iº

Ah! to_ see a - gain the star - tled look,

The maid - en blush, the down - - cast lids, As grow-ing years with sweet sur-

prise _____ did_ hint at love's em - pire!

No chill-ing thought of re-com-pense,___ no chill-ing thought of re-com - pense.___

laid blight up-on her soul!

How blest the days of this com-mu - nion! How sweet the hope, the

hope_____ of some-thing dear - er still!___

(violently)

E. Who would have dreamed that Syl - vi - a was a

fff   cresc.

W.   Walter *mf*

E. flirt,   a vi-cious flirt?   At

f   10

W. least,   she will not wed   me,   she

mf

W. will __ not __ wed __ me   out of grat - i - tude!

Edward

Wed? And does he wish to wed? A man comes bold to woo that means to wed!

Walter (throwing off the mask of indifference)

It is true! Some Don Juan pursues his wicked course!

Edward

E - ven though she's not mine,

I must pro - tect at least our guest, And that rude

churl, who - ev - er he be, shall an - swer to me!

Walter *mf*

The maid seems half a - fraid!

Flute

W. Some oc-cult pow'r, some oc-cult pow'r may be at

W. (excitedly) work! It is time that this should end! Let's have at

W. him! Fair vir-tue we'll de-

Edward

Fair vir-tue we'll de-

(A sudden panic seizes Sylvia and Beatrice at the approach of Edward and Walter.
They rise quickly, keeping their faces hidden, and run down the steps, only to be caught
at the bottom. Edward seizes Sylvia roughly by the arm, Walter bars Beatrice's way.)

care!   We pun-ish a knave   that hides be - hind_ a cloak!

(Sylvia stands still)

Waiter (to Beatrice) *drammatico*
a tempo

Al - tho' you've scorned my_

a tempo
(to Beatrice)

Al - tho' you've scorned my_

a tempo

molto rit.

mf

ff

love,_   I will not see you duped like

ff

love,_   I will not see you duped like

p cresc. molto   *ff*   *mf*

W. *ff* this!

R. *ffz* this!

p cresc. molto *ff* *mf cresc. ed accel.*

(Sylvia tears off her wig and Beatrice lowers her fan; they laugh merrily, while the men start back in

rit. molto Sylvia *p* Allegretto grazioso

S.

Who is duped?

rit. molto *fff* *p*

surprise)

S.

6 6 6 Oboe 6 6 6

(in a conciliatory mood) *p*

S.

It is but a play, a lov ers'

6 6 6 6 6 6

mer - ry, tan - gled knot that I

en - - meshed!

Blame me!

Edward

(throws out his arms to Sylvia)

Blame me!

I al-most let the gold of life run thro' my i - dle fin -

gers! Be mine! I love you, Syl - vi - a! I love you! None

will I wed but you!

(Sylvia falls into his arms)

(Meantime Walter pleads to Beatrice

(for her love)

Agitato (one beat to each measure)

Walter (to Beatrice, recklessly)

I want your love, my Be - a - trice! ___ I will not

have your grat - i - tude! ___ I want your heart, I want your

heart, ___ your love, ___ your soul, ___ your

self! ___ I love you! ___

Beatrice (with quiet intensity)

a tempo

I have found you as the riv-ers find the sea, their home;

a tempo

tude!

a tempo (Edward leads Sylvia towards the rose-bushes and picks some roses and hands them to her

tude!

a tempo

with endearing words)

I____ trust you as the babe its moth-er sweet, its

world! I give all my days, my

Quartet

"Fair youth wove a web of rose-color"

can - o - py!

can - o - py!

can - o - py!

can - o - py!

(as from a distance)

Oh! wing - ed winds,

Oh! wing - ed winds,

Oh! wing - ed winds,

Oh! wing - ed winds,

CPSIA information can be obtained
at www.ICGtesting.com
Printed in the USA
BVHW041207071118
532427BV00021B/424/P